# When You Lose *Someone Special*

*Lance Wubbels*

HARVEST HOUSE PUBLISHERS
EUGENE, OREGON

Cover and interior design by Chris Gilbert, Studio Gearbox
Cover and interior images © tofutyklein; Dedraw Studio / Shutterstock

For bulk, special sales, or ministry purchases, please call 1-800-547-8979.
Email: CustomerService@hhpbooks.com



When You Lose Someone Special



Published by Harvest House Publishers
Eugene, Oregon 97408
www.harvesthousepublishers.com

ISBN 978-0-7369-9154-4 (hardcover)

Library of Congress Control Number: 2025936304



**Printed in China**

25 26 27 28 29 30 31 32 33 / LP / 10 9 8 7 6 5 4 3 2 1

There are no words,

*only tears.*

*"There is a sacredness in tears,"*

said Washington Irving.
"They speak more eloquently
than ten thousand tongues.
They are messengers of overwhelming
grief and unspeakable love."

*"Jesus wept."*
*Have two words ever been more profound?*

When He saw the raw pain of Mary weeping over the death of her brother, Lazarus, He felt His own intense sadness and anger. In that moment,

*even the Son of God had no words.*

Jesus sat down with Mary,
*put His arms around her,*
and wept such a great shower of tears

that the stunned
onlookers exclaimed,
*"See how He loved him!"*

That is the very heart of God.
*Jesus knows our tears,*
shares our griefs,
feels and enters into our sorrows.

Nothing comes close to the
*enduring pain*
and loneliness of the loss
*of someone special,*

someone whom
*you can never replace,*
someone who has been an
intimate part of your life.

The deeper your love,

*the deeper your pain.*

The grief you feel is yours alone,

*different from anyone else's grief.*

To feel as if no one
has ever been through
*what you're experiencing is normal.*
No one has.

Give yourself permission to mourn,
*to feel your loss,*
to fully express your grief,
*without putting a time limit on it.*

The passageway through
*grief is uncharted,*
unpredictable, and messy.
To feel lost and like you are
*going in circles*
is just part of the journey.

There is no formula to use

*or guidelines to follow*

that will fix your grief.

It's not something
you control or manage.
*The love and memories are stronger*
than death and refuse to be stuffed
in a box and hidden away.

There are no magical words

*that will bring you back*

to the life you knew

*with your loved one.*

*How do you live now?*
What is the way through
*the emotional and mental fog*
of loss and pain?
*So many questions*
without answers.

If you can find the
words for the questions
of your heart and
*say them out loud,*
it will help the wound
begin to heal.

It is perfectly normal to feel *heartbroken, angry, and a dull,* aching aloneness . . .

even when you're surrounded

*by friends and family.*

You close your eyes,
*but you can't sleep.*
You feel physically drained.
Time crawls, coupled with a vague dread
for the days to come.
*Your heart and soul and mind ache.*

"Am I going crazy?"

*you ask.*

No. You're grieving.

Where is God in the
midst of your suffering?

Know that in your darkest moment, Jesus is saying, "*I am Immanuel, God with you. Come to Me, just as you are,* and I promise to give you rest. Just come now."

How is it possible that
*the world didn't stop spinning*
when yours did?

How dare the sun keep rising
and the birds keep singing
when your heart is shattered
and your life
*will never be the same?*

Flowing like a stream,
*life goes on as normal*
with no respect for your loss.

Neighbors smile and wave,
*children laugh and play,*
even as you stare out the
window with weary,
unseeing eyes and, at times,
unreasoning resentment.

How do you put your
*life back together*
when all the broken pieces are
*scattered here and there?*

How do you get back
*that part of your life*
that was buried with
*your loved one*
and the future with them
that is no more?

How do you deal with
*the waves of pain*
and memories that ebb and flow
*unbidden and unannounced*
and leave you drowning?

When the weight of grief squeezes
*the life out of you,*
be kind to yourself.
*Go ahead and let it hurt.*

There is no weakness

*or shame in sorrow.*

Jesus wept with the same tears
that drop from your eyes.
Let the tears flow freely and openly.
*The day is coming*
when tears are not so necessary,
*but not today.*

Understand that your loss is a soul
wound, the deepest of gashes to
your mind and heart,
*the worst of emotional hurts*.
Be wise and attend to your wound
and do what the
healing process requires.

Grief takes as long as it takes.

Give yourself a lot of
*grace and space*
and refuse to set
*unrealistic expectations.*

Some people will

*subtly, or not so subtly,*

pressure you to

*"be over"*

your grief.

It's easy to put on a brave mask for them,
*to smother your grief and pretend you're okay,*
but you won't be able to breathe.

As time passes, society will attempt
to silence the real you—the fearful you,
the lonely you, the insecure you,
*the broken you—*
as though you should feel normal by now.
To silence grief only
*intensifies the loneliness.*
To keep talking about
your grief and love is healthy.

*It is okay to not be okay,*
to feel weak, sad, and depressed,
to be angry and scream.

There will be brighter days ahead,
*peace will slowly*
*soften the heartache,*
but today
the tear-soaked tissues remain.

It's natural to try to ignore
*or resist the painful thoughts,*
emotions, and memories that come,
but that only slows the healing process.

Be open to facing your feelings,
all of them,
to not look away
*even when it hurts.*

Grief is not something you
*rise up and defeat*
with sheer willpower.
*It is something to embrace and tend.*

To feel that you're falling apart,
*that your walls have caved in,*
that you can't bear it,
*and everything is out of your control*
is normal.

Why so much pain?
*Your heart is still full of the love*
you knew but cannot now give.
*It's a healthy response*
to immeasurable loss.
*The pain dims with time*,
but not your love.

You can't fill the empty
*chair at your table*
or the empty space
*in your heart and world.*

You can't mend the torn threads in the fabric of your mind and soul.

Step by step, tear by tear,
*moment by moment,*
one prayer at a time,
*one day at a time,*
your heart will slowly
*mend and smile again.*

*Find a friend or loved one*
*who understands your heart,*
who listens with acceptance,

with whom you can
*safely vent your*
bottled-up emotions.

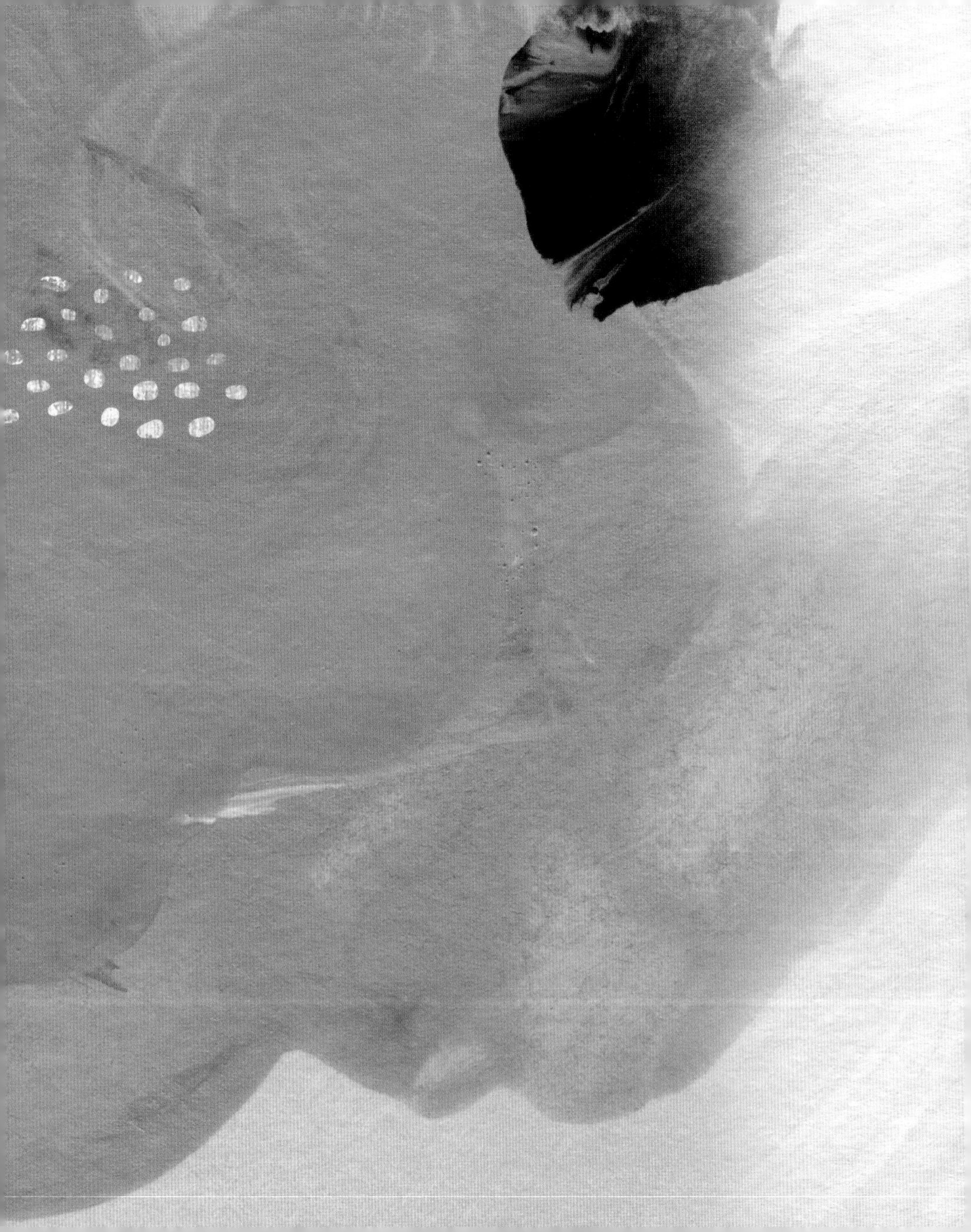

Find companions
*who will walk with you,*
share the pain, and catch a
*few teardrops in their hands.*

*It's okay to question God.*
Mary and Martha questioned Jesus about why He didn't come sooner and heal Lazarus.

He didn't shame or silence them,
*and He won't do that to you.*
He comforts and embraces
*and restores.*

*Feelings of hopelessness*
suddenly slam you at the
*most unexpected*
and unwelcome moments.

It's scary to move forward
when you don't know
what forward means
and you
*feel stuck in what was.*

It takes time
to find your way through
this confusing maze of grief.

*Much has ended,*
much has changed,
*but new life slowly emerges*
from the rubble of loss and pain.

Like anger,
regret and guilt
are common companions
of grief.

We all have things we
did or didn't do that
*we wish we could change.*
Guilt is a heavy burden to carry,
and God's gift of forgiveness is for you.
*Peace comes when you can release it*
and forgive yourself as well.

There may be many reasons why a friend or loved one seems to

*avoid you,*

doesn't call,

*or doesn't mention your loss.*

They may be uncomfortable with
grief and their own sadness
*or simply don't know what to say*
and fear saying the wrong thing,
*so they go silent and withdraw.*

Inevitably, someone who loves you
*and wants to make you feel better*
will offer an emotion-dismissing cliché,
*such as "Time will heal."*

It may be hard to
overlook the innocent,
sometimes hurtful things people say,
*but most people mean well.*

When some people ask you

*how you're doing,*

you realize it's merely

*a social courtesy*

and not an offer to listen and care.

*It's okay to say,*

"It's hard, but I'm dealing with it,"

and leave it there.

If you're feeling disoriented,
*confused, and disorganized,*
even minor decision-making can be difficult.
Have some trusted friends
whom you can call for advice and wisdom,
then make your decision.

Reflections and memories
*of your loved one,*
all the good and the bad,
*the joyful and the painful times,*
remain as a sacred space of comfort,
*a refuge in the storm of grief.*

Relive your memories

*as often as you need.*

Feelings of grief are
invitations to remember, honor,
and celebrate the one you've lost,
*not to forget.*
Even if others don't understand
why it still hurts,
it matters to you.

Anniversaries, birthdays,
holidays, family days,
or other milestones
*may stir up a surge of memories*
that can be difficult.

It’s okay to make room
for feelings that are
magnified and spend those days
in ways that are
*comforting to you.*

There is no return

*to what you knew as normal.*

Recovery is from the intense distress of grief.

*You will carry both your love and pain*

with you and find a new normal.

The Good Shepherd
*will lead you beside waters of rest*
and restore your soul.
*He will take you safely*
through the valley of shadows
and heal a little more
inside you each day.

You will come through this,
with a fading scar
as a reminder of
what was precious
and forever treasured.

## *About the Author*

Lance Wubbels is the author of *I Wish for You* as well as many bestselling gift books with Hallmark. He is also the author of several award-winning books, including *To a Child Love Is Spelled T-I-M-E*, *One Small Miracle*, and *In His Presence*. With more than 40 years of experience in the publishing industry, Lance has been blessed to work with such notables as Joel Osteen, T.D. Jakes, Max Lucado, and many more. He and his wife make their home in Minnesota.